Strength Dreams

Dreams Visions Harmon

sions Harmony Mind Spirit

Spirit Wisdom Streng

Wisdom Strength Dream

armony Mind Spirit Wisd

ind Spirit Wisdom Stren

Wisdom Strength Dreams

reams Visions Harmony M

sions Harmony Mind Spir

from a grain of sand

to a great mountain

all is sacred

- Peter Blue Cloud, Mohawk

armony Mind Spirit Wisd

Mind Spirit Wisdom Stren

Wisdom Strength Dreams

Dreams Visions Harmony M

isions Harmony Mind Spir

Background text (repeated, faint): Strength Dreams Vision Dreams Harmony Visions Harmony Mind Spirit Spirit Wisdom Strength Wisdom Strength Dreams

Travis
name

7/11/2022
date

Paintings by Fritz Scholder

Cover: Plains Dancer, 1995

Harmony: Red #2, 1994

Mind & Spirit: Santa Fe Indian, 1973

Strength: Red #19, 1994

Wisdom: Red #6, 1995

Dreams & Visions: Indian with Orange Headdress, 1995

Copyright 1999 Turtle Island, Inc. & American Indian College Fund

Journal and Chapter Introductions by Wayne Martin & Isabel Summers

Designed by G&G Advertising

Published by Turtle Island, Inc.

300 Mercer Street, New York City, NY 10003

www.turtleisland.com

for American Indian College Fund

ISBN 1-928816-05-3

Sources for Quotations:

Native Time: A Historical Time Line of Native America, by Dr. Lee Francis III

New York, St. Martins Press, 1996

Native Wisdom by Joe Bruchac

New York, Harper Collins, 1995

Words of Power- Voices from Indian America

Edited by Norbert S Hill, Jr (Oneida)

Copyright 1994 American Indian Science and Engineering Society

Printed in Hong Kong

Mind and Spirit
a journey within

Paintings by Fritz Scholder

In the Hopi creation story, Spider Woman

creates life by singing- one word at a time.

The creative power of the word shapes

our very existence. These words arise out

of the Earth and speak of the connection

between all living things. They become

the stories and the songs that define us

as a people and bind us together.

Our Words give us the power to realize our

dreams and visions, bringing harmony to the life

that we envision for ourselves. Words are gifts

inherited from our ancestors - many voices from

the past that through our pen become the future.

Writing releases the voices that are

alive within us. Through writing we are

able to explore our inner self and to find the

wisdom, strength and understanding

that will guide us on our path.

Harmony

The Earth is our Mother.

She nourishes us.

All living things are connected

and we share an equal relationship

with the Earth and all her creatures.

It is from this connection

that we come to understand

the power of Nature and the

importance of living in Harmony

with the Earth and one another.

Show respect for
other living things
and they will respond
with respect.
-ARAPAHO PROVERB

The earth is our
mother. She nourishes
us. That which we put
into the ground she
returns to us.

-BEDAGI (WABNAKIS)

To be in harmony with all things, you must first be in harmony with yourself.

—Lakota Proverb

It is the sacred duty
of every human being
to protect the welfare
of Mother Earth from
whom all life comes.

—Oren Lyons,
Onondaga Nation

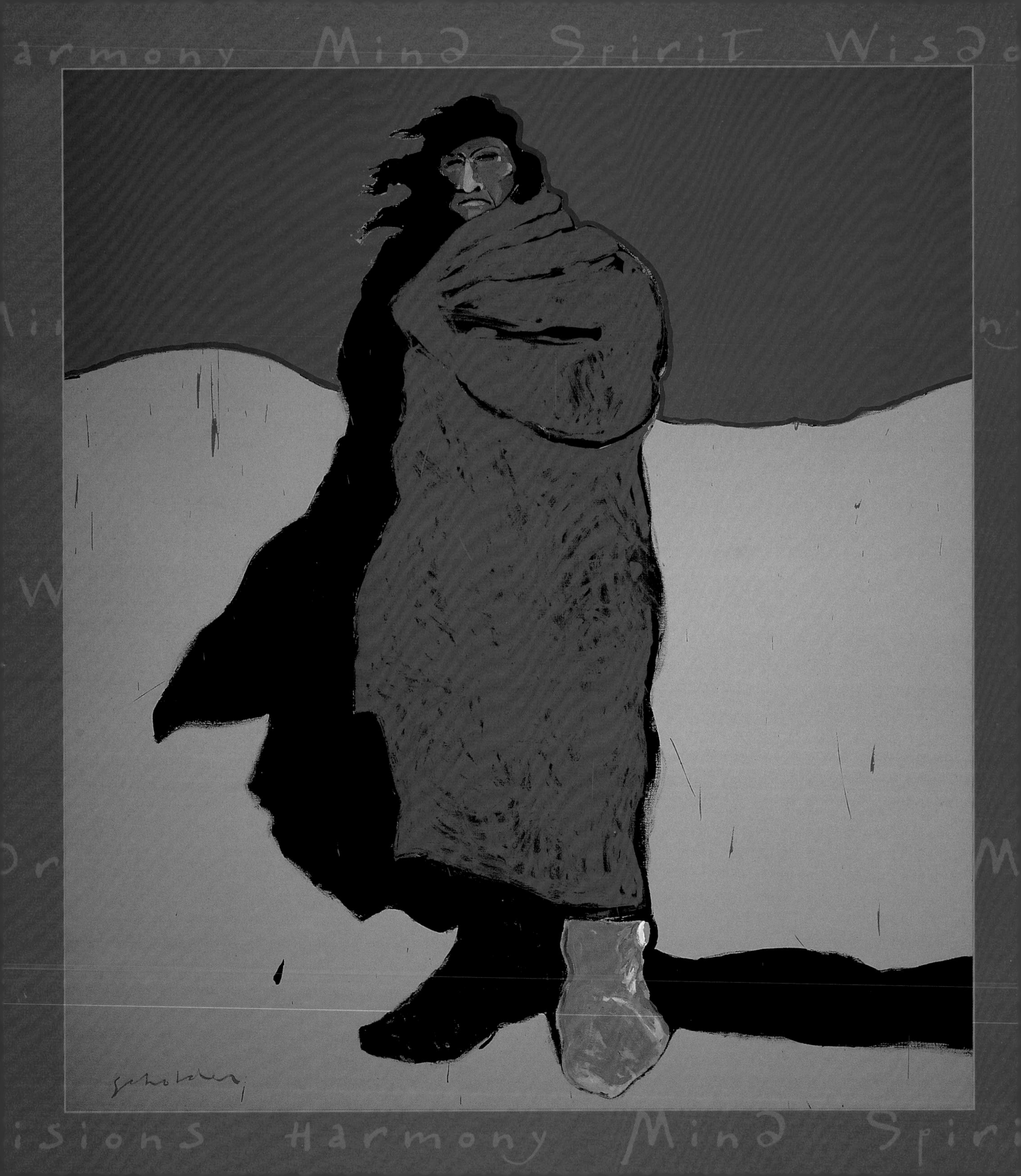
armony Mind Spirit Wisd
isions Harmony Mind Spiri

Mind & Spirit

Being Spiritual begins with the mind

and is about connecting with our inner self.

it is about how we relate in the world.

it is allowing our Mind and Spirit

to guide our motivation.

This is called walking the Spirit Road.

Let your every step

be as a prayer.

—CREEK PROVERB

When many people
live together and
each one cares
for the rest, there is
one mind.

-SHINING ARROWS, CROW

Life is as the flash
of the firefly in the
night, the breath of
the buffalo in
the winter time.

-BLACKFOOT PROVERB

Do right always.
It will give you
satisfaction in life.
–ONONDAGA PROVERB

Treat all humans alike.
Give them all the
same law. Give them
all an even chance to
live and grow.
-Chief Joseph, Nez Perce

Strength

Strength is not only physical,

it is also mental.

Fundamentally it is Spiritual.

The source of our Strength comes from

the guiding principles

we receive from the Creator.

The greatest of these

is that we are all related.

A single twig breaks,
but a bundle
of twigs is strong.
-Tecumseh, Shawnee

Show respect for all
men, but grovel
to none.

-Tecumseh, Shawnee

It is not necessary
that eagles
should be crows

-SITTING BULL,
HUNKPAPA LAKOTA

Winds may blow
strong in my face, yet
I will go forward and
never turn back. I will
continue forward
until I have finished.

-TEEDYUSCUNG, DELAWARE

The greatest
strengths
are gentleness
and kindness.

-MOHAWK PROVERB

Wisdom

You will not have Wisdom

until you have self knowledge.

Strength, Understanding, and Peace

are found only through A Journey Within.

By learning how to live

we bring meaning to our lives

and to those we touch.

If we wonder often,
the gift of knowledge
will come.

-Arapaho Proverb

Knowledge is
inherent in all
things. The world
itself is a library.

-Chief Luther Standing Bear

Life is not separate
from death, it only
looks that way.
-Blackfoot proverb

Give me knowledge
so that I may have
kindness for all.
—LAKOTA PROVERB

If you are to be a leader, you must listen in silence to the mystery and the spirit.

-Leaf Dweller, Kaposia Sioux

Dreams & Visions

By emptying ourselves physically,

we open our minds to Dreams and Visions

that will help direct our life.

In silence and in quietude

Spirit moves to fill the space we have made for it.

The Great Spirit

does not give this to us easily.

One must be of strong

Mind and Spirit to

receive and understand their guidance.

Sometimes dreams

are wiser

than waking.

-BLACK ELK OGLALA SIOUX

The Great Spirit is
generous. He has
allowed you to see
all of life in a dream.
He grants this
to only a few.
-CHEJAUK, OJIBWAY

You cannot harm
one who has
dreamed a
wonderful dream.
-MOHAWK PROVERB

In the old days the
elders tested their
dreams, and in
that way learned
their own strength.

—CHIPPEWA PROVERB

Dreams are wiser

than men.

-OMAHA PROVERB

Educating The Mind and Spirit

The American Indian College Fund raises funds for scholarships and other urgent needs of students at thirty tribal colleges. The colleges were founded by Native Americans to help fight high rates of poverty, educational failure and cultural loss. Run for and by Native Americans, the colleges currently serve more than 26,000 students, representing 250 native tribes each year. The colleges play a vital role in the future of Native American people, and ultimately, in the future of all people.

Please call 800-776-FUND to learn more about the American Indian College Fund where we believe in Educating the Mind and Spirit.

National Headquarters:
8333 Greenwood Blvd.
Denver, CO 80221
1-800-776-FUND

East Coast Office :
21 West 68th Street, Suite 1f
New York, New York 10023
212.787.6312

www.collegefund.org

Native American Artist Fritz Scholder (Luiseno), was born in 1937 in Breckinridge, Minnesota and currently resides in Scottsdale, Arizona. He is a painter, sculptor, and printmaker of international acclaim. Mr. Scholder has been the recipient of numerous awards over the last thirty years including fellowships from the Whitney Foundation, the Rockefeller Foundation, the Ford Foundation, the American Academy of Arts and Letters Award in Painting, and awards from the Salon d' Automne in Paris and Intergrafix in Berlin. In 1966 Mr. Scholder received the Visionary Award from the Institute of American Indian Arts, one of the thirty member colleges of the American Indian College Fund. He has been an Artist in Residence at Dartmouth College and a guest artist at many other educational institutions.

Mr. Scholder received a Bachelor of Arts Degree from California State University-Sacramento and a Master of Fine Arts Degree from the University of Arizona. He has received an Honorary Doctorate of Fine Arts Degree from Ripon College, Concordia College, the University of Arizona, The College of Santa Fe and the University of Wisconsin.

Mr. Scholder has been the subject of eleven books, three PBS documentaries and is listed in Who's Who in America and Who's Who in the World. His work is represented in many public collections including the Museum of Modern Art in New York, Bibliotheque National in Paris and the Smithsonian Institution's National Museum of American Art in Washington, D.C.

armony Mind Spirit Wisdo

ind Spirit Wisdom Stren

Wisdom Strength Dreams

reams Visions Harmony M

sions Harmony Mind Spiri